D1516000

Baby Elephants

ALICE TWINE

PowerKiDS press

New York

For my father, who built snow elephants

Published in 2008 by The Rosen Publishing Group, Inc.
29 East 21st Street, New York, NY 10010

First Edition

Editor: Amelie von Zumbusch
Book Design: Julio Gil
Photo Researcher: Nicole Pristash

Photo Credits: Cover, pp. 1, 9, 11, 13, 15, 17, 19, 21, 23, 24 (bottom left, bottom right) Shutterstock.com; pp. 5, 7, 24 (top left, top right) © Artville.

Library of Congress Cataloging-in-Publication Data

Twine, Alice.
  Baby elephants / Alice Twine. — 1st ed.
      p. cm. — (Baby animals)
  Includes index.
  ISBN 978-1-4042-4148-0 (lib. bdg.)
  1. Elephants—Infancy—Juvenile literature. I. Title.
  QL737.P98T885 2008
  599.67'139—dc22
                                      2007023214

Manufactured in the United States of America

Contents

Elephants are the world's largest land animal. A baby elephant is called a **calf**.

4

African elephants are one kind of elephant. They live in the forests and **savannas** of Africa.

Asian elephant calves live in India, Nepal, and Southeast Asia. They have more hair than African elephant calves.

Elephants are huge animals. Even baby elephants are big. Newborn elephants weigh more than 200 pounds (90 kg)!

11

Elephants pick things up with their **trunk**. They bring food and water to their mouth with their trunk, too.

13

Elephant calves drink their mother's milk. When they are about one year old, calves start to eat plants, too.

Elephants often cover their **skin** in mud or dirt. This keeps their skin safe from bugs and the Sun.

Elephant calves live in family groups. All the elephants in a group help care for an elephant calf.

This calf is learning to use its trunk. Calves need to learn many things. Luckily, elephants are smart.

21

Older elephants teach calves where to look for water. Elephants travel far and wide to look for water.

Words to Know

calf

savanna

skin

trunk

Index

Web Sites

Due to the changing nature of Internet links, PowerKids Press has developed an online list of Web sites related to the subject of this book. This site is updated regularly. Please use this link to access the list: www.powerkidslinks.com/baby/eleph/

24